REFINERY29

STYLE STALKING

REFINERY29

STYLE
STALKING

CHRISTENE BARBERICH + PIERA GELARDI

POTTER
STYLE

This is dedicated to our readers, who truly are the ultimate muses in making it happen and always inspiring us with their infinite smarts and unconventional style moves.

An extra special thanks to Philippe and Justin, our R29 founding partners in crime. To our amazing family, friends, and global R29 community for supporting and encouraging us, and, most of all, challenging us. And to the ultimate Refinery29 All-Stars who REALLY helped build and bring this incredible book across the finish line: Kate, Gabriela, Sara, Mark, Camaren, Caroline, and Connie.

Copyright © 2014 by Refinery29
Photographs copyright © 2014 by Refinery29 except as noted on page 192.

Published in the United States by Potter Style, an imprint of the Crown Publishing Group, a division of Random House LLC, a Pengun Random House Company, New York.

Library of Congress Cataloging-in-Publication Data is available upon request.

ISBN 978-0-8041-8553-0
EBook ISBN 978-0-8041-8554-7

Printed in the United States of America

Book and jacket design by Gabriela Alford
Photographs by Mark Iantosca
Additional photography acknowledgments can be found on page 192.
In collaboration with Connie Wang and Kate Hyatt

10 9 8 7 6 5 4 3 2
First Edition

FEARLESSNESS IN FASHION
GOES A LONG WAY

CONTENTS

FRIENDS (AND PRETZELS) 4 EVER...

BY CHRISTENE BARBERICH & PIERA GELARDI

More than a decade ago, Piera and Christene met while working at an indie magazine functioning (illegally) over a bar in SoHo. They didn't realize it then, but their wackadoodle ideas of what true, memorable, distinctive personal style was all about—white majorette booties! Kooky '60s caftans!—began over late nights of brain-storming, vodka gimlets, and way too many bowls of pretzels. Today, at Refinery29, they're still collaborating, eating pretzels, and making up their own rules—creating a world, every day, that celebrates the coolest, weirdest personal style out there.

Christene: We've been planning this book for two years now...it's honestly surpassed my wildest dreams. What's the most important message you hope readers will get from Style Stalking?

Piera: We've always wanted to do a book together, since Day One of launching

C: That it becomes a constant companion. I want women to read it and feel included, like this is their personal manual for getting dressed for anything, feeling more equipped to push the limits, and ultimately take their style mojo to the next level.

"You only live once, so why not just go for it?"

Refinery29, and here it is—finally. For me, I just hope people walk away feeling inspired to take a risk with their style. Fashion can be so fun and confidence-boosting when you get past this perception of exclusivity or judgment.

C: No judgment! It can take a while to process it, but to really embrace your style, you can't be driven by what other people think. You only live once, so why not just go for it?

P: Definitely. What's the one thing that would make you feel like the book was a success?

P: I think because we're in the process with our readers, we've gone through all the exercises of the book, we can totally relate...it's really US in this book, you know?

C: Yes, totally...it's about these little breakthroughs. And you and I both have them every few years. I think these shifts in how we see ourselves and what we like to wear to express that are super important to acknowledge — in your life and your closet. It inspires A LOT of closet purging. Are you going through a breakthrough now?

P: I do think I'm going through one now. I'm actively trying to take risks and be a bit more expressive with my dressing. But that goes in waves...some days when I'm tired and it's raining, I fall back into a safer space.

C: I feel you...

P: I have to say, it's been really amazing watching your fashion sense evolve throughout our friendship. As someone 10 years younger, you've really inspired me with the fact that you keep getting cooler year after year. I don't think you've ever been more stylish than you are now!

C: Well, that makes me want to cry. And you know, the feeling is mutual. I have to credit you for always activating that ageless spirit in me...being around you and getting to collaborate with you has been one of the biggest gifts of my career.

P: You have so many closet treasures, but you're also a relentless closet purger...is there anything that you'd never let go of?

C: Definitely. This vintage long white Chloé vest, a very old pair of black pony hair Alaïa heels, and these vintage Karl Lagerfeld trousers that were also a gift and are seriously like the perfect cropped baggy pant. I would put them in a safety deposit box if it meant they'd be secure forever!

P: Haha! I know those pants and I don't put it past you.

C: Okay switching gears, what do you think your old lady look will be?

P: Ooh...I love to imagine what different friends will look like when they're in their advanced style years. I want to wear turbans...maybe even have pink hair. I like the idea of bringing out lots of color, pattern, and accessories. I imagine at that point in life, I'll have lost all my hangups and be done with giving a shit what other people think about me—the ultimate style liberation!

C: Here, here....being a decade older than you, I'm rapidly approaching that level of self awareness. I can totally see myself wearing printed Rachel Comey tent dresses and Clergerie platforms on my deathbed! But you know, speaking of old ladies in training, I can also see you're vibe translating to the twilight years! Whenever I'm shopping, you're a bit of a muse to me, as I'm always seeing things I think would look amazing on you. You gave me a lot of courage when it came to playing around with prints.

"I imagine at that point in life, I'll have lost all my hangups and be done with giving a shit what other people think about me—the ultimate style liberation!"

"Style Stalking should give you some handy tools to be your best self...go out there and just wear it!"

P: Mixing prints is like the ultimate rebellion!

C: It feels like a million years ago since we cooked up that infographic on How to Get Shot By the Sartorialist...in the early days, street style had such a signature look in terms of what photographers were drawn to. What do you think is special about street style now?

P: Well, I think the biggest way it's grown and changed is that it's a real business now. When we go to Fashion Week, the pack of photographers snapping attendees is almost as noteworthy as the show we're going to see. Whereas it was once a way to observe and capture a moment in time on the street, it's now so much more intentional. But is that good or bad?

C: I think it's both, but really, the root of street style is just personal style and independent choices. Doing it yourself, without a stylist, flying by the seat of your pants, and just going for it. That's what I love so much about the early days.

P: Fashion Week has certainly turned the dial WAY up on street style...but I tend to really just love people watching when it's not the biggest fashion event of the year.

C: Agree, just spotting cool combinations and unexpected pairings is super inspiring...that's honestly what Style Stalking is all about. So, what do you think non-fashiony women who love style can learn from the looks we've captured in our book?

P: To experiment and have fun! I think we've also chosen a lot of looks that are probably divisive...looks that might not be traditionally "chic." That's something I love about The Book. I think if you're afraid of "making mistakes" you miss the point of style as an extension of self and of life!

C: If nothing else, Style Stalking is a great reminder everyday to be your best self...go out there and just wear it!

P: Amen.

BRIGHTS

There's something to be said about the woman who'll always opt for a punched-up Schiaparelli pink instead of a little black dress. She's adventurous, sure—and probably a little averse to blending in. At the root of it, a brights girl is an optimist. It's a philosophy that doesn't just end with your outfit. Why choose basic anything when you can *shine* instead?

But don't think that wearing bright colors is as simple as ditching your neutrals. A true color fiend knows that pulling it off elegantly is about understanding where to rev things up and when to dial it back. Whether you're going full throttle with color blocking or relying on just one piece to pump up your outfit, using color bravely is one of our favorite things about getting dressed. Period.

So dig out those rainbow-colored hues, those neon handbags, and definitely your most audacious lipstick. We're celebrating brights in the next few pages, and the closet curveballs to making electric shades work for you.

BASIC TRAINING

Bring on the basics in five simple steps.

①

A prim, feminine piece like this lace pencil skirt is a classic, through and through, which makes it the perfect way to integrate a bright. The traditional shape and texture of the skirt complement this color to a T.

②

With bold colors, you can either pile on the hues or hold back to allow one item to really pop. In this case, we love how the other elements are just a simple palette of black and white.

③

If you're more of a minimalist and looking to use color, opt for saturated pastels. They're striking and they deliver a big impact with little effort.

④

Brights have a tendency to look one-dimensional, so don't forget to try them with some texture! Lace is the perfect vehicle for this shade of Pepto pink.

⑤

Brights can be dressed up or down, and while a pink skirt like this could be perceived as fancy, the basic neutrals give it an everyday vibe that's totally unique.

A full-on brights outfit takes some guts to pull off, but in a shorts suit, it's playful *and* manageable.

A coordinating two-piece is already pretty fashion-forward, so make it feel deliberate by choosing a suit with a modern, up-to-date shape. The trapeze-style shorts and cocoon-like jacket with bracelet sleeves offer a totally fresh feel.

"A full-on brights outfit takes some guts to pull off."

Don't be afraid to go big with accessories, too. Adventurous sunnies and an oversized bag will crank your outfit up to the next level.

For statement pieces that speak volumes, it's a good idea to forgo jewelry. Piling it on can be distracting (and not in a good way).

Do keep a part of your outfit basic, though. A plain white tee grounds this stand-out look perfectly.

STYLE MOVES

A basic black coat pales in comparison to this lime green stunner.

If you're going for bright outerwear, stick with a more classic shape. This sleek topcoat makes the green feel more luxurious.

For bold-colored coats, choose a piece that's either long and lean or cropped and boxy. A billowing coat can be overwhelming, and a shrunken version can feel too young (and out of date).

We love a coat in matte, heavy fabrics like wool and tweed. But shinier materials like leather and plastics can end up looking garish. (Not *always* a bad thing in our book.)

SHAPE SHIFTERS

With a neutral outfit, go big with your accessories. This oversized candy-wrapper clutch plays off the volume (and quirkiness!) of a ballerina tutu.

PAST PERFECT

Casual sneakers first emerged in the nineteenth century for vacationing at the beach.

1 PIECE, 3 WAYS

THE BOXY TOP

A structured crop top might not seem like the most versatile piece, but there are myriad ways to wear it, especially when it comes in a stunning Yves Klein blue.

Black and blue do go together. Play up the pairing with cropped palazzo pants and a little leather jacket. Cap-toe pointed stiletto booties and a boxy shoulder bag bring in some graphic pop.

Surprise! This look actually consists of only a collared dress worn under the top. The boxiness of the shirt gives some shape to the full skirt, plus the shirt gives the dress's collar a pretty contrasting canvas. Neutral-hued accessories like this tassel necklace (which actually came from a curtain set!) and oxfords really play up the blue.

③

If you're going to mix your brights, stick with a three-color palette. Sunny yellow and fuchsia complement this blue (yep, they're all opposite each other on the color wheel).

RULE BREAKERS

THIS PAGE: Who says you can't wear a party skirt during the day? Dress it down with a basic oatmeal sweater (the two-toned sleeves on this particular version are next-level). Pretty patterned pumps work for the office, but a pair of lace-up oxfords can be sublime, too.

OPPOSITE: Don't be afraid to dress in a single bright color from head to toe. Bold leggings match just-as-bold tees and statement flats. Scared of looking too neon? Tone it all down with a love-worn leather jacket.

BRIGHTS YEAR-ROUND

WINTER

If you're timid about brights, pastels are an easy place to start. A soft pale pink overcoat is an unexpectedly elegant substitution for white.

FALL

Avant-garde pieces in a palette of black and white can sometimes feel standoffish. Bring in some whimsy with one colorful basic, like this blazer.

IN ALL FOUR SEASONS (AND THOSE WEIRD IN-BETWEEN TRANSITIONAL ONES, TOO), BRIGHTS ALWAYS LIVEN UP A LOOK.

SUMMER

The one color that makes any color really P-O-P? Bright white. In this case, an already high-wattage tangerine shines even bigger and bolder against white accessories.

SPRING

A bright's best friend is a flash of metallic. Whether it's with a pile of necklaces or the hardware on a frame bag, some shine helps give bright pieces more dimension.

SOLANGE KNOWLES

She's got a velvety voice and some serious dance moves, but it's
Solange Knowles's all-her-own personal style that makes us want
to play dress-up in our closets.

What are three items you think every woman should try in a bright instead of a neutral?

"A turtleneck, a plain T-shirt, and a simple leather bag."

You're so daring with color. Is there a shade you just can't stop wearing?

"I can't say no to yellow, fuchsia, or a solid clean white. Someone sent me an online collage that shows how much I've worn yellow and solid white over the past couple of years. It was pretty funny, and slightly embarrassing, to look at."

Do you adhere to any style rules when you're dressing in color?

"When I shot 'Losing You' in Cape Town, one of the Sapeurs—who are experts in all things stylish and elegant—told me never to wear more than three colors at once. I've broken that rule on more than one occasion, but I do think limiting the amount of colors sometimes lends a certain sophistication that dressing like a Crayola box doesn't. But sometimes looking like a Crayola box is more fun!"

"I communicate through color. It simply makes me happy."

What are your favorite color combos that provide a killer one-two hit?

"That's a tricky one for me. I almost don't have one or two! All primaries just seem to work, and all pastels just seem to work. I recently wore Pepto pink with blue and orange, and that unexpectedly turned out pretty well."

When it comes to bright makeup looks, what's your philosophy?

"Go for a bright lip or a bright eye, and keep everything else neutral. In a photo shoot with lighting, this rule is meant to be broken, but in everyday life I haven't seen anyone pull that off—other than Lupita Nyong'o, who pulls off basically everything!"

You're a true-blue globe trekker. What colorful places have inspired the way you dress?

"Senegal, Rwanda, Ghana, Mexico City, Jamaica, Morocco, and my new home, New Orleans. I've gotten such beautiful pieces from all these places that really reflect the way I've evolved in my personal style."

What do you love most about wearing brights?

"I communicate through color. It simply makes me happy."

ZOOM LENS

With vibrant hues so electrifying, a brilliant swipe goes a long way.

Smart layering indulges two opposing surges. First is the let's-wear-everything-all-at-once proclivity (nope, it never goes away). Second is our obsession with functionality. Let's be honest: There's just nothing more useless than a jacket or a dress we can wear only one way. Layering allows us to accomplish more with our clothing while working with less, and, ultimately, to stretch the limits of our closets. Being able to wear one piece three ways is just the beginning. Layering lets you shoot for three *hundred* ways!

Existing cross-genre, cross-trend, and cross-season, smart layering is the most practical trick in the styling toolbox. It can serve you even as your tastes transition throughout your lifetime. But even more so than with other styling skills, layering without finesse is a surefire way to look schlumpy. To help you master layering (and avoid looking slapdash), we offer some guidelines and tips from women who really know how to pile it on.

BASIC TRAINING

Five tips for cozying up to lots of layers.

①

Don't feel compelled to wear only winter coats in the winter. Two lighter fall jackets can provide just as much warmth.

②

The key to good jacket Jenga is getting the shapes right. Always layer the shorter, slimmer one underneath.

③

To make layered jackets more purposeful (and interesting), pull the inner jacket's lapel over the top layer.

④

Avoid mixing too many patterns. One solid bright print and one subdued shade provide a nice balance.

⑤

When your coat game is taking the lead, keep the rest of the silhouette simple.

If you're going to have one basic shirt for layering, make it a classic white oxford. In soft cotton, stiff poplin, or loose linen, this piece is totally indispensable.

One of our favorite things to do with this piece is to layer it under a simple sweater. Choose something with a crew neck for a more modern feel.

"With so many layers, it's important to keep your accessories on the leaner side."

Especially in a monochromatic outfit, a white shirt can be striking. And don't tuck it in! A curved hemline can help define your waist and make you look long and lean.

To build on this simple layered look, find a beautifully constructed topcoat that hits you at mid-thigh. Unfastened, it adds a great longer layer to the pants-and-shirt combo.

Remember that with so many layers, it's important to keep your accessories on the leaner side. A pouch clutch and wedge boots are no-nonsense but still infinitely cool.

STYLE MOVES

An all-white look is so much more interesting when layers are involved.

Start with a basic piece that's got some volume. A slub-knit sweater, for example, is slouchy but still holds its shape.

A full goddess-draped skirt mimics the pleats on a schoolgirl uniform but is a lot more grown-up.

Button it up with a little structure in the form of a sharp trimmed collar.

PAST PERFECT

Gabardine, the material originally found in trench coats, was invented by Thomas Burberry for the military in 1901.

SPLURGE OR SAVE

Many vintage trench coats have sleeves that are far too wide. Snip them off for a budget-friendly DIY!

1 PIECE, 3 WAYS

THE LITTLE LACE DRESS

A pretty, feminine dress can be worn with so much more than just heels. Here are three ways to layer it up while dressing it down.

(1)

The easiest way to layer this dress is with a tailored jacket. A leather moto topper looks good, but we like it here with a single-button blazer paired with fun everyday sneakers.

(2)

Turn your dress into a skirt with a sweater and a blanket scarf. Knee-high boots and leather-look leggings offset the frill of classic lace.

(3)

Find a stiff pleated skirt that's longer than the dress. This will add some volume to the skirt, and you'll never have to worry about your "top" coming untucked.

RULE BREAKERS

THIS PAGE: When you're layering a structured jacket with an oversized sweater, it's best to pick a sweater that's got some length to it. That way you won't end up feeling frumpy on top.

OPPOSITE: Skirts-over-pants might feel wrong, but when done right, it's so, so right. Choose a pant that's got some length and a skirt that's on the flowier side for a proper mix of proportions.

LAYERING YEAR-ROUND

WINTER

We have a tendency to overlayer in the winter, but if you're scared of looking like a marshmallow, just make sure to keep it lean on your bottom half.

FALL

When working with lots of lengths, try starting with your darkest color as your first layer and gradually going lighter to your top layer.

SUMMER

In summer, go for light, breathable layers like chambray and linen. Just keep the proportions long on top and cropped on bottom (or vice versa) for maximum breeziness.

SPRING

Create a de facto cape by wearing your outermost jacket around your shoulders. It will cut that early spring chill.

NATALIE JOOS

Natalie Joos is the intrepid stylist and founder of the blog Tales of Endearment, not to mention a street-style superstar in her own right. Inventive layers just happen to be one of her (many) strong suits.

As a stylist, is there a difference in approaching layering when putting together an editorial look for a magazine versus putting together an outfit for yourself?

"Layering is a trick stylists use a lot in order to get all our designers and credits in. It's also very visual, so you can create all these great, beautiful shapes and silhouettes. Layering is like composing—it lets you put a little story together. It's fun creating a balance, whether the story is about matching—through prints or colors—or clashing—again, through prints or colors."

"Layering is like composing—it lets you put a little story together."

Are there references that you find yourself always tapping into when you layer?

"I'm really inspired by the way men layer, with their shirts and vests and sweaters and blazers. In the fall, I love layering coats over blazers."

What's one layering item that you feel yourself gravitating to time and time again?

"I love my striped T-shirts. I recently bought this super-worn, destroyed vintage shirt, but it looks great with everything. You can put a blazer over it, or wear it over a dress or a collared shirt."

ZOOM LENS

Mastering the perfect pile-up means knowing when to add *and* subtract.

Some people misconstrue *ladylike* as "stuffy"—or, even worse, "boring." In our book, dressing in a ladylike manner has nothing to do with how many shades of pink your outfit consists of, or how many skirts hang in your closet. Modern feminine dressing is all about maintaining a balance between softness and sleekness. Just as every rose has its thorn, every *good* ladylike outfit has its own sharp surprise.

Whether you're dressed in *Mad Men*–type frocks or menswear-style trousers, the ladylike approach comes through mostly via silhouettes. Meant to create a shape that exaggerates a trim waist and long legs, ladylike pieces are typically high-waisted, fuller around the hips, and cropped to show a flash of ankle. A lady will pick up that vintage graphic T-shirt at a thrift store, but she'll wear it blouse-like with a pleated A-line skirt and pointed D'Orsay pumps.

It takes some know-how to strike that perfect proportion of shape, color, and accessories. Here's how to ensure that your own brand of ladylike always looks punched-up, never (ever!) prissy.

BASIC TRAINING

How to pull off ladylike nudes in five easy-to-mimic steps.

(1)

The simplest trick in the ladylike book? A (slightly messed-up) ballerina topknot. Teamed with a wine-stained lip, it's the daytime version of a black-tie updo.

(2)

Look for well-constructed, lace-accented blouses in thrift shops. These work with a variety of outfits and look so chic when tucked into a high-waisted skirt or jeans.

(3)

Wearing super-high heels means keeping your skirt length in check. A longer hemline (even in a miniskirt!) prevents your outfit from looking too leggy.

(4)

Our brand of ladylike means pairing pretty pastels with in-your-face accessories. Here, contrast counts big!

(5)

There's no shoe more leg-lengthening than a nude-hued pointed-toe pump. No need to go for four-inch stilts, though—even a kitten heel can visually add inches to your bottom half.

A boyish oxford gets feminine with some punched-up hues. Salmon and cherry red color blocking is a totally unexpected spin on a ladylike blouse.

Ladies tuck in their shirts, but don't be scared to rough it up a bit. A more relaxed tuck takes the stiffness out of an outfit (and it's how your blouse ends up during the day anyway, isn't it?).

"Salmon and cherry red color blocking is a totally unexpected spin on a ladylike blouse."

A small box bag doesn't have to feel precious. With a longer strap you can throw over your shoulder, a mini satchel is supremely functional.

A knee-length slim-fit skirt doesn't equal stuffy. In a wild retro print, it can be a statement piece (that just happens to be a thrift-store staple).

Knee-high boots get an anti-dominatrix treatment with thick soles, a roomy shaft, and a swipe of lipstick-red trim. It's a pretty, feminine shoe that still feels cool.

As for jewelry, a lady never skimps. Delicate shapes and matching metallics allow you to wear earrings, necklaces, and bracelets all at once.

STYLE MOVES

How does a modern lady pull off blazers and a button down? Think: clean layers, short hems, and whimsical accessories.

When it's cold out, we can deal with heavy tights only so much. To switch things up, try a pair of cozy thigh-high boots in a skinny, formfitting suede; they're slimming and a tad sexy.

There's no bag quite as appropriate for the modern-day lady as an underarm clutch, and we love picking them up as souvenirs while on vacation. This Moroccan–style version brings a bit of souk-steez to an otherwise demure outfit.

A double-breasted coat can make you feel like a Wall Street Robber Baron, but in an ultra-tailored hourglass cut, it can be the most alluring thing you own.

SPLURGE OR SAVE

Patterns tend to go in and out of style pretty quickly, so opt for a budget version. In a busy print, less pricey fabrics can be camouflaged!

SHAPE SHIFTERS

Make sure trousers end right above your ankles. It's a tiny touch that transforms a pantsuit look from corporate to couture.

1 PIECE, 3 WAYS

THE WHITE LACE SKIRT

Whether full and swirly or tight and pencil-length, a white lace skirt can give any outfit an old-world glamour that transcends trends. It's a ladylike essential that will always have a place in your closet.

(1)

A vintage silk jacket plays off the luxuriousness of lace, while the bomber shape and cobalt blue hue crank up the fun factor.

(2)

Tuck a crisp white oxford into the skirt for a ladylike spin on menswear dressing. A felt fedora and a leather-stamped box bag add some offbeat Annie Hall to the mix.

(3)

A vintage tee, a cropped moto jacket, and heeled ankle boots are a busy girl's staples, but the mermaid hemline in sweeping white lace makes everything feel completely fresh.

RULE
BREAKERS

THIS PAGE: A ladylike tone is all about silhouette, so look for body-flattering shapes in soft knits, light velvet, and silk for a feminine finish.

OPPOSITE: When your outfit is on the vampy side, delicate accessories like chain bags and cap-toe pumps are all you need to keep things classy. Slimmer heels, more jewelry-like hardware, and richer fabrics are just the thing to complement a body-con skirt.

LADYLIKE YEAR-ROUND

WINTER

A clean-cut black topcoat provides the perfect counterpart to a more voluminous winter skirt. Plus, you'll wear it all winter long!

FALL

With rich textiles like tweeds and leathers, a topcoat can have loads of personality but still look polished. Use it to anchor a full skirt and a simple blouse.

TAKE YOUR LADYLIKE VIBE FROM HOT TO COLD AND BACK AGAIN BY BANKING ON A FEW KEY PIECES.

SUMMER

The polo shirt might seem like a preppy-jock throwback, but its structure and shape are 100 percent ladylike. We love wearing it on top of a knee-length dress for a new Gatsby vibe.

SPRING

This is the time to debut the ladylike dresser's most powerful piece: the floral frock. Go for broke in a dress that mixes patterns and recalls a retro silhouette.

CAROLINE ISSA

Consultant, publisher, and style maven Caroline Issa always
has the ladylike look of our dreams, even if she's wearing a
men's oxford and vintage jeans.

What's the one thing in your closet that you own too many of?

"White shirts. Classic, tux-style, silk blouses, oversized, cropped—you name it, I have it. But a white shirt can be the base for many an exciting outfit!"

For the modern girl who wants to pull off ladylike, what are three things she could invest in?

"A tuxedo for evening, Prada anything, and a pair of Alaïa heels."

"Ladylike dressing will eternally have the same ambition."

What's the finishing item you find yourself constantly reaching for to take your outfits to the next level?

"A swipe of red lipstick and a great pair of earrings always do the trick for me."

Does dressing ladylike today mean something different than it did fifty years ago?

"Ladylike dressing will eternally have the same ambition—to look chic, to give the wearer an air of confidence, and to ensure that the woman wears the clothes rather than the clothes wearing the woman!"

ZOOM LENS

Our kind of ladylike pushes the limits on fierce femininity.

What do corporate queens, suburban goths, Jay-Z, and Parisiennes all have in common? An affinity for head-to-toe "all black everything," to quote the Hov. But if you look a little closer, the thing that connects all these folks runs deeper than just a color. People who wear all black tend to appreciate the same no-bullshit philosophy when getting dressed: power, protection, and interchangeability. Find us someone who's able to get dressed in two minutes (or less) and *still* command a room, and we're 99 percent certain her go-to shade is black.

But to be good at ABE isn't only a matter of owning black wardrobe staples. When you're limited to one color, it actually allows you to be *limitless* in other ways. From shape and texture to accessories and layering, pulling off black effectively requires more creativity than if you have the entire rainbow at your disposal. The following pages showcase a few of the women who do black-on-black every day, and prove just how vibrant and versatile this classic hue can be.

BASIC TRAINING

Five fab steps to fading into black the right way.

(1)

To keep from looking like an usher, it's important to have a strong theme with black clothing. In this case, it's a new kind of urban cowboy.

(2)

A slightly oversized black blazer is a piece that'll serve you throughout your life. Find one in a nonshiny fabric for maximum mix and match–ability.

(3)

Black skinny jeans should be either skintight and cropped or just slightly baggy to avoid that awkward are-those-leggings-or-pants question.

(4)

If you're going for a black boot with a slight Western vibe, choose jeans with a longer hemline. It'll create a rumpled vibe that's super cool.

(5)

A good-quality black fedora can be a lifetime signature. Just choose one that has a classic brim and doesn't look cheap!

If you're planning on creating a pretty silhouette with lots of black layers, it's a good rule of thumb to keep your bottom half on the slimmer side. Here, black tights help anchor the outfit and allow you to really pile things on up top.

When layering with black, play with textures. Leather, knits, crepe, and cottons all pull their own weight.

"It may seem counterintuitive, but including a colorful piece can draw attention to individual black items."

Including a colorful item can draw attention to individual black pieces by breaking up the large swaths of uniform color. The collar and tails draw the eye to the different layers, adding dimension.

Wearing a too-short, full skirt over a pencil skirt is a clever way to DIY a peplum. It's tricky to pull off with colors because the hues can be more difficult to match, but in blacks it's a piece of cake.

When picking the right heeled bootie, find one that stops at the skinniest part of your ankle. Any higher, and you'll end up with cankles.

STYLE MOVES

Resurrect the strapless black top! Here's how to modernize this super-flattering piece.

Avoid heavy '90s connotations by finding one in a more tailored shape (no stretch Lycra!) with some menswear detailing like pinstripes or buttons.

A straight neckline looks more fashion-forward (not to mention daytime appropriate) than a sweetheart or peaked one.

Wear it with trouser pants, a midi skirt, or another item that's got some length for a balanced look that's not as overtly sexy.

BEAUTY BEAT

A decked out
dark outfit can
really pop with just a
swipe of intense red
lipstick—an ABE
girl's best
friend.

EXTRA, EXTRA

You can't ever go wrong
with classic all-black
accessories like a sleek
envelope clutch or a basic
pump—especially when
the rest of your outfit
is all black, too.

1 PIECE, 3 WAYS

THE LEATHER MOTO JACKET

Whether yours is boxy, cropped, skinny, or pleather, a leather-look moto jacket with lapels is a must-own item.

(1)

Over a professional work shift with fancy heels and a clutch, a moto jacket serves the same purpose as a blazer, but looks way edgier (it's warmer, too).

(2)

Push up the sleeves to show off a patterned pullover underneath. Slouchy boots and a leather shopper play up the weekend vibe.

(3)

Wearing a jacket over a longer tunic is a quick trick for an instant outfit upgrade. Here, skinny leather pants and a structured work bag make this 9-to-5 appropriate.

RULE BREAKERS

THIS PAGE: A swingy polka-dot dress can be your sneakiest comfy office outfit. An allover spot might feel cutesy in any other color, but in black, it's pure Rei Kawakubo cool.

OPPOSITE: When you're wearing all black, playing with proportion is just as important as texture. A cropped shirt and a below-the-knee-length skirt are devastatingly sexy but don't feel too obvious. These two examples of the same concept prove that the best accessory to a snappy look is a partner in crime!

BLACK YEAR-ROUND

WINTER

Update the beatnik uniform of turtleneck, leggings, boots, and a leather jacket with something totally off-the-wall in an all-black wardrobe—pink!

FALL

A classic black lace dress is an autumn essential and looks extra chic worn under your standby moto.

IF THERE'S ONE COLOR THAT'S A YEAR-ROUND GO-TO, IT'S BLACK. HERE'S HOW TO MAKE THE MOST OF THIS INSANELY VERSATILE SHADE.

SUMMER

A so-deep-navy-it's-basically-black feels vibrant but still matches all your black favorites. Wear with pumps for a dressier take on a summer day look.

SPRING

Mixing patterns with black is a cinch. Just stick to classic prints like leopard and plaid and tuck them into breezy high-waisted shorts.

NORMA KAMALI

After 40 years in the business, this fashion designer is still creating
the most in-demand essentials for millions of women.
No wonder her favorite everyday color is black!

On a practical level, what most draws you to black?

"It's great for travel. It's great for family events. It's great for your professional life. It's incredibly versatile. Sometimes—and this is unfortunate, but this is how it is—bringing too much attention to your wardrobe presents you as less substantial, and more about style than function and performance. There's something really incredible about the neutral quality and power of black."

"There's something really incredible about the neutral quality and power of black."

Why do you think black holds such cultural significance, especially for women?

"When I was in Abu Dhabi, I went to the Grand Mosque and interviewed the youngest female minister in the Middle East. I asked her how she felt about having to wear an all-black abaya to work. She said that when she's in an abaya, men can only listen to what she has to say. They're not looking at her butt or her breasts. They see her hands, they hear her words, and they look at her face, and she said that she can get the job done so much more easily. Her face was *illuminated* in that black. It was like a frame for her eyes and her intentions. For me, I think that a Little Black Dress can do the same thing and send the same message."

ZOOM LENS

Basic black? Never! This complex shade is your ultimate calling card.

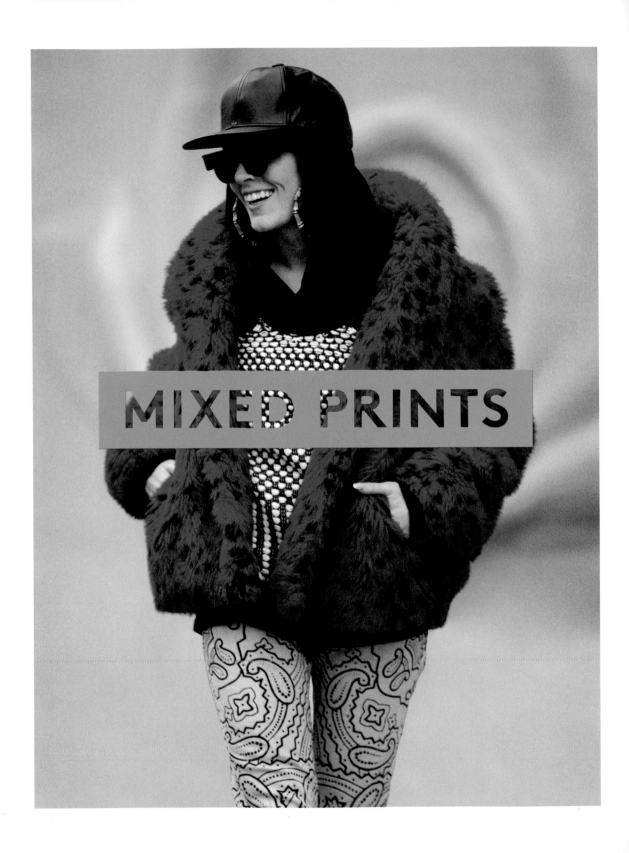

Although it literally involves nothing more than putting two items together, many gals out there (present company included) feel intimidated by mixing prints—and for obvious reasons. For every chic, inventive combo cooked up, there are a dozen haphazard pairings that feel about as elegant as a Lou Reed–Metallica mash-up.

But here's the thing: It may seem like a gamble, but mixing patterns is a pretty formulaic skill. And once you've figured out the equations, the payoff can be astronomical. The trick is all about finding the common denominators through color and making sure scale, genre, and size are well balanced.

Even if math isn't your strong suit, we're sure that the reward—a killer original outfit—is well worth the effort you'll need to get there. For a cheat sheet on acing mixed prints, take a look at these one-of-a-kind outfits. They all prove that in fashion, just a little bit of crazy-pants goes a long way.

BASIC TRAINING

How to stir the prints pot in five simple steps.

①

When playing with patterns, it's always good to have one anchoring item, like a coat or a pair of trousers. The black jacket here pulls it all together.

②

For your printed pieces, look for items in simple, no-fuss shapes like a shell crop top and tapered trousers.

③

Mixing prints in different color families may seem wacko, but it can totally work. Just look for the connection, either in the style of print or in a single color that travels from pattern to pattern (here, it's pink).

④

In general, prints should contrast in at least two ways. For these, the mix happens with the color and the "randomness" of the print. The toile print is laid out in neat, recurring patterns while the floral shirt is chaotic.

⑤

A nude pump, even in a crazy pattern, tends to read as a neutral, so feel free to go wild!

One easy way to mix prints is to stick to the same color story for all your patterned pieces. Looking for an easy place to start? Mixing black and white is a no-fail combo with loads of versatility.

When layering prints this way, the first tip is to find two pieces that each have the alternate color as the dominant hue. The polka-dotted blouse is mainly white, while there's more black in the jacket.

"Pairing random prints can look haphazard, but the best rule of thumb is: Trust your gut."

Logically, it doesn't seem like two busy prints can work together, but sometimes, like here, they can create a layering effect that seems intentional and chic. Pairing random prints can look haphazard, but the best rule of thumb is: Trust your gut.

Denim is always a great, neutral anchor that keeps your prints in check. Here, a little distressing mimics the animal print of the jacket, but isn't overwhelming.

STYLE MOVES

Here's how to make a patterned pencil skirt look anything but corporate.

The common denominator between the two prints is a floral theme, but the large recurrent paisleys and the allover ditzy Liberty print balance each other out.

Prints can make items look larger than they really are, so it's important to go slimmer and shorter whenever possible. A bit of skin between the tied-up blouse and the skirt acts as a visual palate cleanser.

Your jewelry factors in, too. A jumbled-up collection of textured, multi-colored seed beads is as much an interesting "print" as any of the other pieces.

EXTRA, EXTRA

In our book, a graphic leopard print is a neutral. It complements any other print, whether it's a check or a stripe (or even another leopard!).

SHAPE SHIFTER

A slouchy shirt and a soft jacket call for a skirt in a structured shape. This origami-folded mini provides just the right juxtaposition.

1 PIECE, 3 WAYS

THE SOFT, PRINTED BLAZER

Easily thrifted or found in mall shops for a song, this cheap thrill can offer big-ticket inspiration.

(1)

It takes guts, but a beautiful vintage-look skirt and a cutesy graphic-heart jacket are contrasting pieces that really balance each other. Try wearing with a solid-colored tank and loafers.

(2)

Though these four prints feel very different, they tell the same pop-art, graphic story, which is why this hodgepodge works so well. Also, how clever is the big red heart bag?

(3)

When you're pairing like prints (the miniskirt swaps yellow Barts for red hearts!), it helps to wear one solid-colored piece that bridges the two. In this case, the vest acts as a stylish centerpiece.

RULE BREAKERS

THIS PAGE: When wearing large swaths of printed fabric, try to find prints that are bigger in scale, too. Photorealistic smiles, jumbo plaids, and a Bauhaus zigzag are the kind of opposites that attract (and we dig it).

OPPOSITE: Mix prints *and* some shine. A metallic paisley skirt paired with a silky floral-striped shirt is like a Kelly Wearstler pad made wearable.

MIXED PRINTS YEAR-ROUND

WINTER

A textured coat with a wide weave is a print unto itself. Wear it with not-so-basic skinny jeans.

FALL

One of our autumn staples is the long-sleeved dress. Here, a psychedelic-printed frock gets tempered by a pop-art sweater.

IF YOU'RE THE TYPE WHOSE IMAGINATION NEVER GOES ON HOLIDAY, MIXING PRINTS IS ON YOUR AGENDA 365 DAYS A YEAR.

SUMMER

An easy way to casually introduce prints is through your add-ons. Camo and checkerboards are a snap to match and go with loads of colors and genres.

SPRING

Mixing crisp black-and-white prints *always* works. In this case, a chessboard cardigan with a prison-stripe skirt suit looks super cool, and way more unexpected for spring than a floral.

SUSANNA LAU

One of the most fearless pioneers in the digital space (not mention the street-style scene), Susanna Lau—along with her blog, Style Bubble—is the gold standard for audacious dressing.

Why do you think mixing prints is such a scary thing?

"I think that people who are generally scared of drawing attention to themselves stay away from mixing prints, but I just don't really *care*. Small children might be laughing at me on the tube, but it makes me happy."

What is the craziest print that you currently own?

"I've got these pieces by this graduate-school designer named Beth Postle with a Picasso-style face portrait. She's done it in all these tops and bottoms that I think are so fun to wear together."

"Getting dressed is so much more about satisfying a personal whim than getting dressed for other people."

Do you have any motivators for when you get dressed?

"I don't have this thing about 'good taste' that people need to adhere to, and a level of chicness. I just don't believe in any of that. My thing is that I just really love wearing all of my clothes at the same time. For me, getting dressed is so much more about satisfying a personal whim than getting dressed for other people. Those whims and themes and moods, though, are more like 'I want to dress like autumn leaves' or 'I want to channel Elizabeth Bennet' than looking sexy or slim or pulled-together."

ZOOM LENS

Sometimes the most brilliant mash-ups are also the most soft-spoken.

For most of us, denim is ground zero in terms of personal style. From the first big designer purchase you ever made to the first thing you reach for when your outfit mojo is running low, denim is fashion's universal starting point. Unlike any other item, your jeans are steeped in history. They transcend trendy and have the uncanny ability to blend into the background or totally make your outfit. The takeaway: Denim is the ultimate chameleon.

For these reasons, exploring what makes denim invisible and what makes it stand out is key to really taking advantage of its magical powers. From dressing head to toe in denim (hello, Canadian Tuxedos!) to making your everyday jeans feel not so basic, this chapter is dedicated to celebrating the hardest-working pieces in your closet—and getting them right day after day, year after year.

BASIC TRAINING

A five-step guide to a foolproof jeans-and-tee getup.

1

For many women, a skinny jean is a must-have. Typically, a darker wash (from true blue to deep indigo and black) is the most elongating.

2

When it comes to distressing, a little goes a long way. If you want a bit of wear and tear on your everyday pants, don't go further than a few small rips on the pockets and knees.

3

To tuck or not to tuck? A good rule of thumb: If your shirt's on the tighter end, keep it tucked in. Anything looser deserves a half tuck at most.

4

With skinny jeans, it's *all* about the ankles. The end of your pant should hit the top of your anklebone to achieve the longest, leanest line.

5

Heels pair as well as flats with jeans. Think about contrast, though. In this case, heels make a T-shirt and backpack feel extra special.

You're looking at one of the simplest, most foolproof combos out there. To give a T-shirt and jeans a fashion-forward spin, focus on shape.

To tween-proof this pairing, go for a boxier shirt and looser-fit jeans. The volume will give you the leeway to go for wilder accessories.

"To give a T-shirt and jeans a fashion-forward spin, focus on shape."

This is the perfect opportunity to reach for a tall, skinny, pointed shoe. Instead of making an outfit look too done-up, a prim pump makes a T-shirt and jeans look sharp, not schlumpy.

The relaxed vibe of the T-shirt and jeans can be offset by a more polished outer layer. We love the dreamy shade of blue in this knee-length topcoat.

Want a little something extra? A flannel tied around your waist provides just a hint of grunge, without looking messy.

STYLE MOVES

A denim shirtdress can be swanked up in three easy steps.

Cuff the sleeves of your shirtdress and undo a few buttons to allow a shipshape striped shirt to peek out from underneath.

Shirtdresses tend to be on the fuller side. Cinch one with a wide belt to play up your curves.

Polished ankle boots are a fail-safe complement to denim shirtdresses. We love little Chelsea boots or vintage lace-ups.

PAST PERFECT

The first jeans makers used indigo dyes, which bind to fibers to create a durable fabric with wear. Hence, blue jeans are blue.

EXTRA, EXTRA

A double-knotted necktie and wide-brimmed hat pay homage to denim's Western roots (but we like wearing ours with heels, too).

1 PIECE, 3 WAYS

THE PATCHWORK JEAN

Whether yours are lightly patched or have that full-blown Junya Watanabe treatment, a patchwork jean is the antidote for dullsville denim.

①

Pulling off an avant-garde pair of pants definitely means being okay with making an impact. This Comme des Garçons paper-doll dress and shell-top sneakers create a combo that's completely unforgettable (in a good way!).

②

A relaxed-fit bottom calls for a fitted, ladylike top. To create a *new* New Look silhouette, cinch a blouse with a good belt to play up your curves.

③

When you're rocking fringe, fray, *and* patches, keep your shoes sexy and your shirt classic. Even in an oversized, boxy cut, this pretty pink oxford ensures the pants look cool, not clownish.

RULE
BREAKERS

THIS PAGE: Denim on denim
(especially when your jeans are in
the same wash and weight) can look
elegant when worn with lingerie-
style tops. Keep both fits on the
looser side for a more laid-back spin.

OPPOSITE: We love an ultra-
destroyed pair of boyfriend jeans
for a subversive take on sexy. Wear
them with your most look-at-me
heels and a boxy blazer for a
nouveau-Parisian ensemble that's
as cool as it is va-va-voom.

DENIM YEAR-ROUND

WINTER

Nail the perfect pile-up with patchwork denim, around-the-waist layers, and lots of pieced-together parts in various hues of indigo.

FALL

Everyone needs a good, broken-in vintage denim jacket. Throw it on top of a darker-wash button-down for an everyday layered look.

CLASSIC DENIM PIECES WILL BECOME SEASONAL STAPLES. HERE ARE A FEW TO RELY ON.

SUMMER

A loose-fit pair of cuffed denim is sunshine-appropriate with a luxe T-shirt, box bag, and barely there sandals.

SPRING

We love a '90s-style bona fide relaxed jean with knee rips. Wear it with high-heeled boots and a boxy top for a fun throwback.

LAURA BROWN

As executive editor of *Harper's Bazaar* and the inimitably charming host of *The Look*, Laura Brown is your best friend next door who also happens to be insanely stylish. Her secret weapon? Denim.

What are the hardest-working jeans in your closet?

"I love J Brand Marias. They're just high enough in the waist without being mom high. Acne jeans have this slouchy thing in front that sort of gives me a pouch that looks awesome. Frame Denim's Le Skinny de Jeanne are also great. Those are my three go-to jeans."

Do you feel a sort of kinship with other women who love denim?

"I find there's a no-bullshit sensibility that my fellow jeans-wearing friends have. I think we share a sort of 'Let's get out the door' mentality. There's so much going on in my head that I can't devote too much time to my outfits."

"I find there's a no-bullshit sensibility that my fellow jeans-wearing friends have."

Story time! What was your first pair?

"My first-ever pair of jeans were probably Levi's 501s. It was like they conjured up the idea of these Peter Lindbergh supermodels who all wore 501s. I wanted to be one of them!"

What's one pair of jeans missing from most women's closets?

"Every woman should own a pair of wide-leg high-waist jeans. They just do wonders for your legs. I actually have a pair that Ali McGraw would have loved. You put them on and instantly your legs look like they go on for miles."

ZOOM LENS

From a casual cuff to a refined fray, the blues have it.

DENIM_0119

GOOD VINTAGE

If there's one thing that separates those with genuinely cool personal style from those who just have big bank accounts, it's the ability to thrift. To go into a department store and leave with a stunning ensemble is one thing, but it's next level to pull it off in your neighborhood consignment store. It takes a strong sense of self and a great eye to do vintage well, and it's no surprise that some of the most stylish women we know count thrifted finds among their closet's most precious pieces.

Just like any current-season fashion item, vintage runs the gamut from cheap thrill to big-ticket score. Best of all, we love vintage because it's all about making it your own. You've got to hunt for it, fall in love with it, and tailor it up. As with any good relationship, that extra bit of effort makes *all* the difference.

Figuring out what makes *good* vintage truly good is key to pulling it off yourself. From building a strong collection of old-school pieces to making your throwback find feel modern and fresh, channeling the past perfectly is all laid out in the chapter ahead.

BASIC TRAINING

Five steps to incorporating vintage pieces without looking dated.

①

Vintage jackets are one of the few thriftable items you can easily wear in bigger sizes. If the sleeves of an oversized bomber are too long, just cuff them!

②

Vintage items always need one up-to-date piece to keep things feeling relevant. The boxy sweatshirt and minimal skirt offer a perfect counterpart to the throwback jacket.

③

When shopping for vintage bags, simple silhouettes and quality materials go a long way. You can't go wrong with a basic black frame bag.

④

A sneaky way to give your thrifted jacket a little extra TLC is to get the lining replaced. Not only will the update feel good against your skin, but it's a way to personalize your piece (ie: choose a bold color).

⑤

We think that wearing vintage with minimal jewelry feels much more now than piling things on. Just a sweet necklace or a plain cuff will do.

One of our weak spots is a good printed thrifted shirt. Avoid cheap materials like polyester, and go for cottons and silks. Wear it with everything from a pencil skirt to beat-up jeans.

It pays to find vintage that's a little oversized. You can always tailor your items to perfect the fit (which just happens to be a surefire way to make something look expensive).

"Find a jacket that's obviously been loved? Even better!"

Some people feel queasy about used shoes, but nothing really holds us back when we spot a gem. Just get them professionally cleaned by a cobbler if you're hesitant.

And guess what? Some of the best vintage finds aren't in the women's departments. Shop men's and little boys' sections for some quirky basics like blazers and button-downs.

Find a jacket that's obviously been loved? Even better! Personal touches like patches, embroidery, and pins are a great starting point for you to add to.

STYLE MOVES

A white lace dress ain't just for that *one* special day.

We admit it: Lots of vintage wedding dresses make great summer sundresses.

Try one with a menswear belt and tough black booties—the contradiction is key.

Go super-short or mid-calf-length and a vintage white dress can become your go-to summer frock.

BEAUTY BEAT

Easy modern hairstyles always match up best with vintage outfits. Go for soft beach waves, not a Gibson Girl updo.

PAST PERFECT

Aloha prints were invented in Hawaii and popularized by World War II servicemen who were stationed in the Pacific.

1 PIECE, 3 WAYS

THE PATTERNED SUNDRESS

There's definitely more than one way to wear a sheer lemon-hello, ruffle-necked vintage sundress (yep, even when it's not summer anymore).

(1)

Don't overthink it. Sometimes you just need to let the dress speak for itself. Wear it with no-nonsense ballet flats, a simple leather tote, and a classic pair of shades.

(2)

For an unexpected nighttime look, a turtleneck, a clutch, and platforms can be dramatic. If you're not brave enough to show so much leg, opt for a jersey miniskirt underneath.

(3)

The length makes for a perfect swingy maxi skirt. Cover up the voluminous neckline by wearing a structured, thicker shirt on top. We like this soft-shouldered blouse, but a worn sweatshirt would work, too.

RULE BREAKERS

THIS PAGE: If you're opting for a head-to-toe vintage outfit, do it with a good mix of timeless and wacky. A boxy moto jacket, a retro-printed shirt, and overalls are pretty much always on trend.

OPPOSITE: Feeling a '60s-style frock? Go all the way and wear it with a colorful pair of tights. With some vintage heels and a thrifted box clutch, this mod getup is daring without looking dated.

GOOD VINTAGE YEAR-ROUND

WINTER

Black is one of the easiest colors to thrift. Pile on the textures and silhouettes for a curated, urbane look that'll help cut the chill, too.

FALL

Definitely retro but ultimately rad, a pair of '80s floral pants can be just the thing to liven up your go-to fall wardrobe of everyday sweaters and blouses.

FROM LIGHT, PRINTED LAYERS TO CHUNKY COATS IN A CLASSIC SHAPE, VINTAGE IS A MUST ALL YEAR LONG.

SUMMER

Make traditional folk pieces work for everyday by mixing them up with a few modern, fashion-forward showstoppers.

SPRING

A pretty vintage dress can work for day or night, especially when tights can be tossed! Just switch out the shoes and add a statement jacket.

SOPHIA AMORUSO

Mega-successful site Nasty Gal started on eBay as a place for
Sophia Amoruso to sell her vintage scores. With deep roots in thrift,
Amoruso's personal style is also tied to the thrill of the hunt.

What makes vintage so exciting?

"I always had an affinity for vintage. I felt it from the first threadbare T-shirt I found locked away at my grandfather's motel as a child. Vintage pieces are imbued with a quality that can't be matched. Vintage is part of a history that we can breathe even more life—and time—into."

What's the first rack you head toward when you're thrifting?

"Outerwear! I've found the best coats and jackets in thrift stores, from crazy anoraks to the perfect three-quarter-sleeved blazer that's always hiding in the little boys' section."

"Vintage is part of a history that we can breathe even more life—and time—into."

Tell us about your most precious vintage treasure.

"I have a pair of vintage John Fluevog shoes that I wore every day when I was eighteen. I wore them so much they broke entirely in half. They are the ultimate elf shoes—I'm working on getting them framed."

For vintage newbies, why is an online dealer like Nasty Gal a good place for resources?

"Each piece we sell is styled head to toe, so if you don't know how to style vintage, we've already done the heavy lifting. I love thrifting, but it requires a lot of time and patience—and a stomach for finding other people's ancient Kleenex in the pockets!"

ZOOM LENS

Make fashion history with a thoroughly modern mix.

In French, it's called *jolie laide.* In polite vernacular, it's *interesting.* But for us, dressing ugly pretty is just plain awesome. For a whole tribe of fashion freaks out there, the goal of getting dressed each morning isn't to look nice, pretty, taller, or slimmer. It's to challenge conventions, deconstruct the style rules, and create a look that feels totally new and personal. If your inclination is to pair a full-length evening gown with platform creepers and a silk bomber, you're speaking our language!

Designer Miuccia Prada has said that "ugly is attractive, ugly is exciting." We couldn't agree more. With a knack for finding the commonalities between a whole slew of genres, trends, styles, and sensibilities, pioneers of ugly pretty are often pegged as the nerds of fashion—and for good reason! If you appreciate Victorian lace, punk booties, and avant-garde silhouettes in equal measure, it takes some brainwork to bring it all together.

And while there are no hard-and-fast rules for breaking the rules, we'll show you—right here!—what trailblazing looks like on the fashion front.

BASIC TRAINING

Bring on the wow (and weird) factor in five easy steps.

①

Get your head(gear) in the game, and pick winter's hardest-working accessory—the beanie—in a nostalgic thick knit with a quirky pom-pom.

②

A kooky pair of sunglasses might seem tricky, but they'll pair with *anything* if it's in a neutral color.

③

A clever way to mix prints is to play with scale. A tiny spray of polka dots looks cheeky next to big, circus-sized spots.

④

Wear your nighttime shoes in the day. A pair of socks in a contrasting color helps dress them down.

⑤

When pulling off wild colors, patterns, and accessories, sometimes it's best to find your core pieces in classic cuts like a long, sleek topcoat and a full, below-the-knee-length skirt.

Ugly pretty is all about finding familiar pieces that have a weird twist, like a classic pair of heeled boots in Jekyll-and-Hyde color blocking.

See that ring game? Choose three adjacent fingers to wear three similar rings on. It's a DIY knuckle duster that won't get you stopped by the TSA.

> ## *"Ugly pretty is all about finding familiar pieces that have a weird twist."*

Certain sweater fabrics, like thick angoras, metallic-foil yarns, and mohairs, can feel retro (in a bad way), but as long as you pair the sweater with slim, modern-cut pieces and a forward-thinking makeup look, it can be totally now-feeling.

The ugly sweater is a hallmark of an ugly pretty wardrobe. Find ugly sweaters in nonseasonal colors (sorry, red and green!) to wear all year long.

STYLE MOVES

Thought sporty pullovers were for Little League players only? Think again.

Whether you go for a real vintage deal or a new version, the fit is key. Anything too baggy or boxy will look like pajamas.

Below, wear a classic cut like a midi skirt or a cropped trouser in a complementary print. It's so much more deliberate—not to mention interesting—than a basic black bottom.

Pair with lots of bold accessories for a layered, more-is-more look.

BEAUTY BEAT

Stick-straight, waist-length, center-parted hair is hardcore elegance with a '70s spin. Talk about super-striking.

SHAPE SHIFTER

A truly special-feeling print deserves to be *seen*. Don't shy away from a statement coat— embrace it and make it your thing!

1 PIECE, 3 WAYS

THE WACKY TROUSER

An out-there pant is more versatile than you think. Freeing you up to go simpler in the other parts of your outfit, a patterned trouser can actually make dressing up *easier*. Here are three ways to wear it without looking, well, *crazy-pants*.

①

Use two of the more neutral colors in your pants' palette to figure out how to layer on top. To take things to the next level, pick one accessory in the same color family, but a whole lot brighter. Who can resist such a happy lime-green shoe?

②

Prints on prints? You know we're down with that. Here, an orderly Swiss dot completes the chaotic swatches of stripes.

③

Feeling nervous? Start off with a basic graphic tee, a slim-fit jacket, and black shoes to let the pant speak (or shout!) for itself.

RULE BREAKERS

THIS PAGE: Pile on your colors, prints, and shapes. One consistent color (in this case, black) will tie everything together—promise!

OPPOSITE: Doing ugly-pretty-*sexy* means including a cheeky element of surprise. A sheer skirt (with hot pants) and a mullet-curved crop top are out there but not obvious.

UGLY PRETTY YEAR-ROUND

WINTER

Arbiters of ugly pretty know better than to get locked into one proper winter coat. Layer different light, wacky jackets every day to keep warm.

FALL

A short-sleeved coat might be impractical on anyone but you. Wear it over one of your (many) patterned blouses.

THERE'S NEVER NOT A TIME TO DRESS LIKE YOU'RE MARCHING TO THE BEAT OF YOUR OWN DRUM.

SUMMER

It's too obvious to wear a dainty shoe with a pretty miniskirt like this. We'll pick the combat boot every time.

SPRING

Full-on prints might feel like mayhem to anyone else, but you know how distinctively chic they can be, especially in luxe materials like silks and satins.

IDIL TABANCA

The founder and editor in chief of *Bullett* magazine opens
up about empowerment, compliments, and why it's better
to always look a little off.

What does ugly/pretty mean to you?

"It's empowering; specifically, it's girl power. You're not putting forward your best assets. It's like an 'F.U.' to everyone. I don't have to show my cleavage or wear body-hugging clothes to be awesome. I can wear the ugliest shit and still be super dope."

What is your favorite unexpected mash-up?

"I like mixing really elegant clothes with more industrial-looking accessories. Every time I have to dress for something and am totally made up, I don't feel like myself anymore. Something always has to be a little

"If I can make you like something that you're normally repulsed by, to me, that's the best."

off. When a normal person looks at me and asks, 'What the fuck is she thinking?,' that's when I start feeling comfortable."

What's the most flattering thing someone could say to you?

"To be perfectly honest, the most flattering thing someone could say to me wouldn't be about my outfit, but if it was, it'd be something like 'I would have never thought to wear that, but it looks great on you.' If I can make you like something that you're normally repulsed by, to me, that's the best."

ZOOM LENS

Real irreverent style takes guts and a "f**k you" fashion attitude.

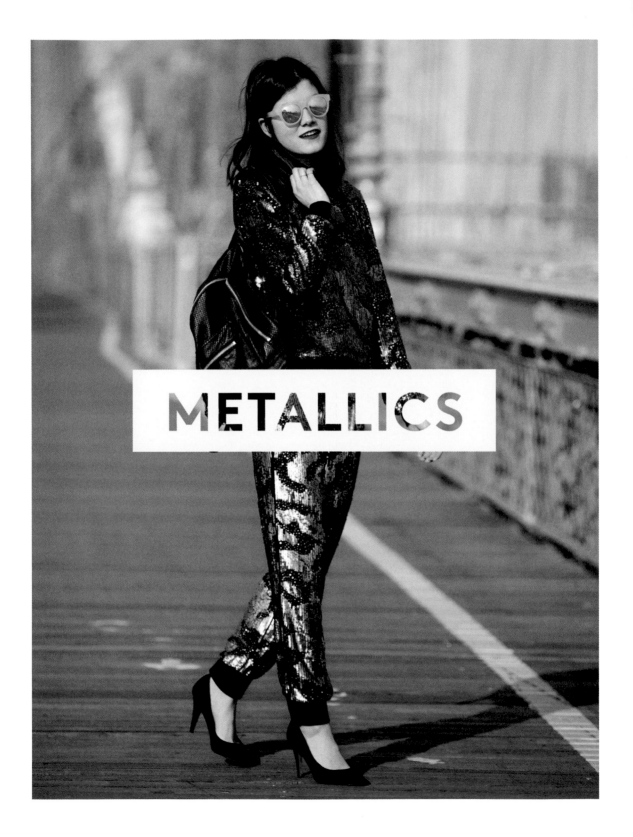

METALLICS

Even the most hardcore minimalist among us has a soft spot for some glint. C'mon, if you're even remotely into clothing, style, and fashion, chances are you've got a magpie hanging out in your psyche. Magpies are naturally attracted to shiny, shimmery treasures, and they collect metallic trinkets with an instinct similar to the one that draws you to every pair of silver shoes imaginable. What can we say? A love of metallics is natural and intrinsic—don't fight it!

Whether you're going for Studio 54 levels of glitz or are just looking to add some bling to your thing, metallic tones are (literally!) a brilliant way to create dimension in an outfit. And those of us who've had the happy accident of finding ourselves in a sunny spot while wearing a gleaming piece know the unabashed joy of discovering we're a disco ball.

In the following pages, we've pulled together a few clever tricks of the trade that'll have you looking like the glamorous glimmer girl that you are. All together now—*ooh, shiny!*

BASIC TRAINING

Five steps to going for the gold.

(1)

How's this for daytime drama? A gold topper works because it comes in a casual cardigan shape, but in a decidedly uncasual material.

(2)

In this brilliant of a shine, a jacket needs to be streamlined, slim, and simple. No shoulder pads, please!

(3)

Underneath, it's safest to go totally casual or totally monochromatic. A wide palazzo pant and a sheer shirt are cinematic but don't feel out of place in the sunlight.

(4)

Pro tip: It's well worth getting a vintage sequined jacket lined. Itchy arms are never worth the shimmer.

(5)

When it comes to accessories, bring in shine through lacquer. A patent clutch and acrylic sunnies can sparkle (but won't steal the spotlight away from your jacket).

A sequin skirt is more versatile than you think. In particular, a pencil-skirt shape is easier to wear than a mini, and it parlays into tons of outfit opportunities.

Find something in a mid-rise, knee-length, and slim (but not skintight) fit. Anything too body-conscious will ruin the rippling effect of sequins. When it comes to shine, you need some wiggle room.

"A sequin skirt is more versatile than you think."

As for sequin size, the smaller, the shinier. You want sequins that catch the light, and a couple thousand do it better than a couple hundred!

Instead of a totally monochromatic outfit (see opposite page), this outfit relies on a crew-neck sweatshirt to balance the sparkle.

As for accessories, veer toward the simple, unfussy side. Peep-toe black platforms and a chain crossbody bag are polished but not prissy.

A little toughness in the form of studded bangles can be powerful. Double them up on both wrists for a look that Wonder Woman would dig.

STYLE MOVES

Metallics for everyday? Hell yeah, you can!

Try to find one statement item like a structured top or a blazer, and stick to neutrals to fill out the rest of your outfit.

Silver is always a safe bet. In some lights, it can look like a slate gray, but once you move, it's way more interesting than a flannel.

Mitigate the shininess of your metallics with matte black items. Whether in the form of wool trousers, a velvet stripe, or a supple leather bag, they'll give your outfit a rich feel that's grown-up and glamorous.

1 PIECE, 3 WAYS

THE BROCADE PANT

Gold-foil pants don't have to be a holiday-only item. Think of them as more rock and roll than Secret Santa.

With a varsity jacket and an Ivy League–approved oxford shirt, a brocade pant trumps your regular skinny jeans.

A long, lean cardigan makes a gilded pant feel boardroom-friendly. A prim blouse and plum-colored pointed heels ensure they are party ready, too.

With a vintage fur coat, a band tee, and kaleidoscopic oxfords, this outfit works in all the right ways.

2

3

RULE BREAKERS

THIS PAGE: Don't be scared to mix your metals. A rose-gold skirt and golden shoes sweeten up an oversized sweater. Go for thicker materials like leather or neoprene, though— anything flimsier can feel a little cheap.

OPPOSITE: A new trend in the metallic landscape is neon-hued fabric in a beetle-bright oil-slick effect. Lucite accessories aren't a metallic, per se, but they're just as refractive and shiny. We think of them as part of the fam, too!

METALLICS YEAR-ROUND

WINTER

Thick, pleated knee-length skirts are a must in the winter, and a copper version instantly takes a preppy uniform to the next level.

FALL

A lightweight Lurex sweater in a pretty mauve color or a metallic bomber jacket makes fall staples way more fun.

SOME FESTIVE SHIMMER ISN'T ONLY IN SEASON DURING THE HOLIDAYS. HERE'S HOW TO WEAR IT ALL YEAR.

SUMMER

Shimmering taffeta doesn't have to read prom. In a starkly minimalist shape, it can be classic and downright elegant.

SPRING

A sheer, sequin-scattered jacket with short sleeves gives a basic black outfit a little flapper finesse.

LEANDRA MEDINE

Author, blogger, and pioneer of the Man Repeller movement, Leandra Medine knows a thing or two about living that heavy metal lifestyle.

What is it about metallics that makes them so interesting?

"Metallics by nature can be harsh, but when they're worn the right way, they can be very tasteful and project a style home run. I find them compelling because they leave so much room to inject personal style."

What's the secret to doing metallics during the day (without looking like you're doing a walk of shame?).

"My rule with sequins is that if I'm wearing them, I also have to be wearing either sneakers or denim."

"All is fair in love and sparkle."

What's your everyday metallics game like?

"I am always wearing a gold diamond pavé snake from my brother's jewelry line on my pinky, and a diamond ring from Turkey that my grandmother gave me. It sort of looks like a vintage engagement ring, but it was actually a gift my grandmother gave to her mother that she got back when my great-grandmother died."

Is it possible to go overboard?

"All is fair in love and sparkle."

ZOOM LENS

A glimmer here, a shimmer there—lose yourself in the shiny stuff.

We've never been ones to acknowledge any sort of division between "girl stuff" and "guy stuff." We like our cheesy action flicks as much as we do our classic rom-coms, and we're just as likely to order a whiskey, neat, at the bar as we are a glass of blubby. Because, really, are we borrowing from the boys if those oxford shirts, pleated trousers, and sports jerseys were ours to begin with?

Today being a "tomboy" isn't as much about repurposing traditional menswear pieces as it is about honest-to-goodness ease, opting for fit instead of fashion, balancing the rigid with the relaxed, and building a long-lasting stable of clothing that'll outlive any fleeting trends. But, of course, the fun part about any style is interpreting these components to match your personality. A true tomboy knows how to make a party dress, a stiletto heel, and even a Pepto pink coat look as effortless as a Hanes T-shirt.

Ahead, we've broken down some inspiration for achieving a modern-day tomboy vibe that's totally gorgeous in guy-ville.

BASIC TRAINING

Beat the boys at their own game in five steps.

①

Even if you don't work in a corporate office, a crisp white button-down is an essential menswear layer. We love it buttoned all the way up, too.

②

When it comes to purses, luggage- and briefcase-style shapes are your bag—literally.

③

To make sure your sweater feels "grandpa-chic" (minus the "grandpa") find one in a timeless cropped version.

④

Snazzy lace-ups can be as dressy as heels. Use them to jazz up a simple outfit.

⑤

Balance out a totally menswear-inspired look by incorporating one traditionally feminine item—in this case, a pair of cat-eye sunglasses. The inclusion will make both sensibilities shine stronger.

Well-fitting overalls are a classic tomboy essential. For a grown-up pair, find one with a cropped, tapered leg and choose a lighter-weight denim with a softer drape.

Underneath, test out a top that shows off your clavicle. A little bit of skin keeps your overalls from feeling too juvenile.

Pant legs still too long? Cuff them! Flashing a sliver of ankle, even in boots, is always flattering.

"A little bit of skin keeps your overalls from feeling too juvenile."

To keep you warm, a longer overcoat creates a boyish shape. In a cheerful red, this topper still feels feminine.

Every girl needs a pair of basic black boots. For a tomboy look, choose a lower heel and a shorter shaft. Ankle boots are the most versatile option.

STYLE MOVES

Bermuda-style knee-length shorts don't have to make you look like a tourist.

Go baggy, but not *too* baggy. You need a little room in longer shorts, but if you're swimming in them, they can look shlubby.

Darker colors are easier to pair. Add some pizzazz with a colorful crossbody bag and a patterned belt.

It's easy to DIY your own pair. Snip a pair of too-short relaxed-fit chinos right above your knees. Voilà!

BEAUTY BEAT

True tomboy style means keeping your beauty routine low maintenance, but a good glow never hurts. A light bronzer and tinted balm are all you need.

PAST PERFECT

The first leather moto jackets were made in 1928 by the Schott brothers, and retailed for just $5.50 apiece.

1 PIECE, 3 WAYS

THE DOUBLE-BREASTED BLAZER

The slightly boxy dapper-dude blazer is a tomboy wardrobe essential. Here are three ways to dress it up.

1

Go for a head-to-toe Annie Hall look with a collared shirt, a cozy cardigan, cropped trousers, penny loafers, and a fedora. No sweat if your navys don't match—it's part of the charm!

2

As the outermost layer of a veritable onion of style, a blazer can give a piled-on outfit some definition. An ankle-length skirt and structured silk layers are a tomboy's take on traditional ladylike pieces.

3

This is a grown-up version of uniform dressing. The white ankle socks give the look a nostalgic spin, especially when peeking out from a pair of vintage-look lace-up boots (another tomboy essential).

RULE BREAKERS

THIS PAGE: Don't hold back! Wear all your favorite tomboy layers (leather, denim, plaids, and cottons) at once. Top them off with your freshest snapback.

OPPOSITE: Play the garçonne game with a simple—but effective—exercise in sharp cuts, in a dramatic blazer, a severe turtleneck, and a portfolio clutch. Even a girlish peplum feels tough in this case.

TOMBOY YEAR-ROUND

WINTER

Forever tomboy shapes like vintage-style topcoats get a pop of energy in a fresh, vibrant color.

FALL

In the fall, your blazer can stay on all day long. Make a point of it, and cinch it with a bold, skinny belt.

INJECT SOME DAPPER DRESSING INTO YOUR ROUTINE WITH A FEW OF OUR FAVORITE GENDER-BENDING BOY-MEETS-GIRL STYLE MOVES.

SUMMER

The onesie is our favorite throw-on-and-go item in summer or, really, any season. Pair it with low-pro sneakers and a cute cap for a modern Newsies vibe.

SPRING

A cropped, lightweight puffer jacket is as chic as it is comfy. Try wearing it with slouchy jeans and cutout booties.

JENNY KANG

Stylist Jenny Kang is responsible for some of the most inspiring outfits you've seen in catalogs and magazines, and her own style is the perfect embodiment of the modern tomboy.

What are the three tomboy pieces you find yourself buying over and over?

"Cropped trousers, blue button-down shirts (a good chunk of my closet), and anything sweatshirt-y."

Many times, menswear is all about the details. What little styling tricks or elements do you rely on to get that look?

"I think being aware of how you want something to fit is super important, as the fit of an item can achieve various looks. If you wear a pair of pants perfectly tailored and cropped, you get more of a boyish feel, whereas an oversized slouchy fit can feel a little more masculine."

"It's always fun to raid the men's department."

Who are some of your tomboy icons?

"Gayle Spannaus always gets that mix of masculine-feminine right on the ball. Her secret is all about tailoring the heck out of your clothes. She can even make a pair of trompe l'oeil sweatpants look sophisticated!"

Who are the go-to designers/ boutiques that you rely on for tomboy pieces?

"I love Sacai right now with their mash-up of menswear and sport. I always find unique and interesting items at La Garçonne, and J.Crew is great for raiding the men's department."

ZOOM LENS

True tomboy style goes way deeper than blazers and brogues.